BIG
book
of Australian
nature

www.steveparish.com.au

introduction

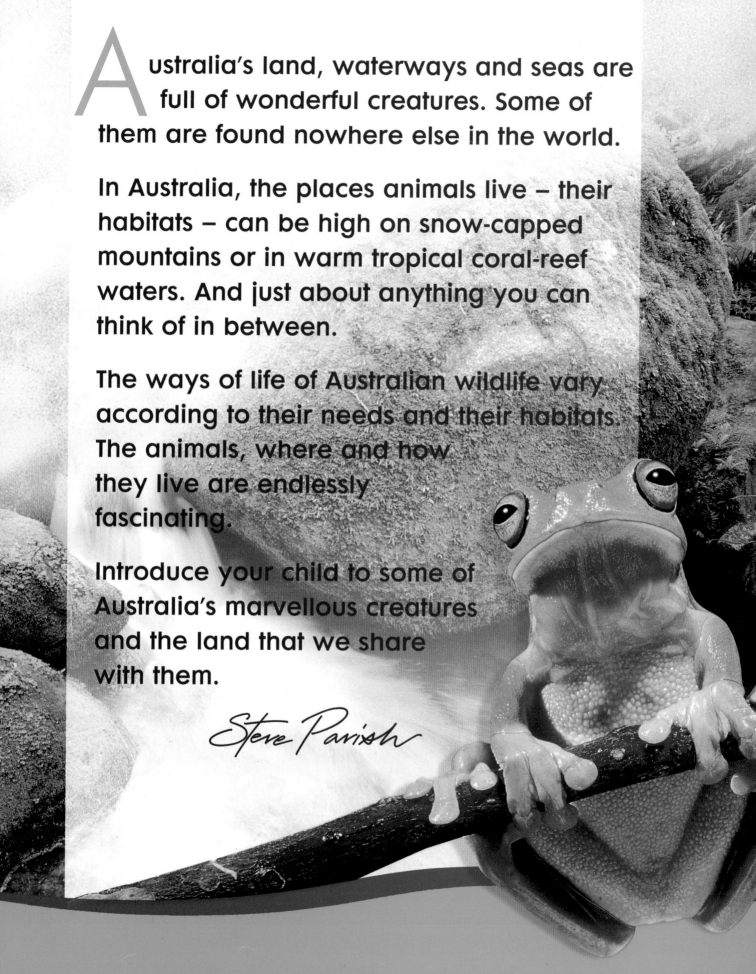

Australia's land, waterways and seas are full of wonderful creatures. Some of them are found nowhere else in the world.

In Australia, the places animals live – their habitats – can be high on snow-capped mountains or in warm tropical coral-reef waters. And just about anything you can think of in between.

The ways of life of Australian wildlife vary according to their needs and their habitats. The animals, where and how they live are endlessly fascinating.

Introduce your child to some of Australia's marvellous creatures and the land that we share with them.

Steve Parish

contents

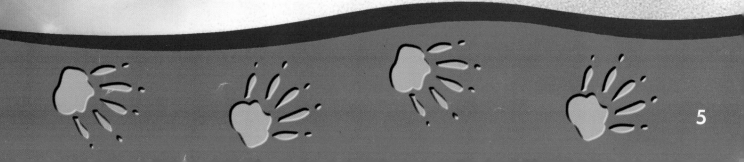

Koala

Koala eats the leaves of gum trees.

Echidna

Short-beaked Echidna has strong front claws for digging.

Mouse

Spinifex Hopping-mouse lives in dry country.

What animals live in Australia?

Possum

Squirrel Glider sleeps during the day in a nest in a hole in a tree.

Kangaroo

Red Kangaroo hops on strong back legs.

Bilby

Bilby carries young in a pouch that opens backwards.

mammals

Cockatoo

Sulphur-crested Cockatoo has a strong beak for cracking seed pods.

Duck

Pacific Black Duck has webbed feet for swimming.

Wren

Red-winged Fairy-wren lives in bushes near the ground.

What animals live in Australia?

Rosella

Eastern Rosella makes a
nest in a hollow tree or
a hole in a fence post.

Hawk

Pacific Baza has
very good eyesight.

Pigeon

Common Bronzewing eats
seeds it finds on the ground.

birds

Gecko

Ringed Thin-tail has no eyelids and licks its eyes clean.

Green Snake

Green Python is hard to see among the green leaves of trees.

Turtle

Saw-shelled Turtle has webbed toes for swimming in fresh water.

What animals live in Australia?

Snake

Taipan is very dangerous to humans.

Lizard

Ring-tailed Dragon runs on its hind legs.

Crocodile

Saltwater Crocodile is a meat eater that will eat anything it can catch, including humans.

reptiles

Yellow and Green Frog

Red-eyed Tree-frog has sticky pads on fingers and toes to help when climbing.

Bell Frog

Western Green and Golden Bell Frog lives near water.

Tiny Frog

Green-thighed Frog is only 4 cm long.

What animals live in Australia?

Calling Frog

Tyler's Tree-frog puffs up his throat to call to females.

Green Frog

Green Tree-frog croaks loudly when it rains.

Bullfrog

Australian Bullfrog's croak sounds like a duck quacking.

frogs

Spotted Fish

Coral Rockcod has bright blue spots.

Ray

Stingaree has barbs on its tail that are venomous.

Seahorse

Big-Belly Seahorse's body is protected by bony plates.

What animals live in Australia?

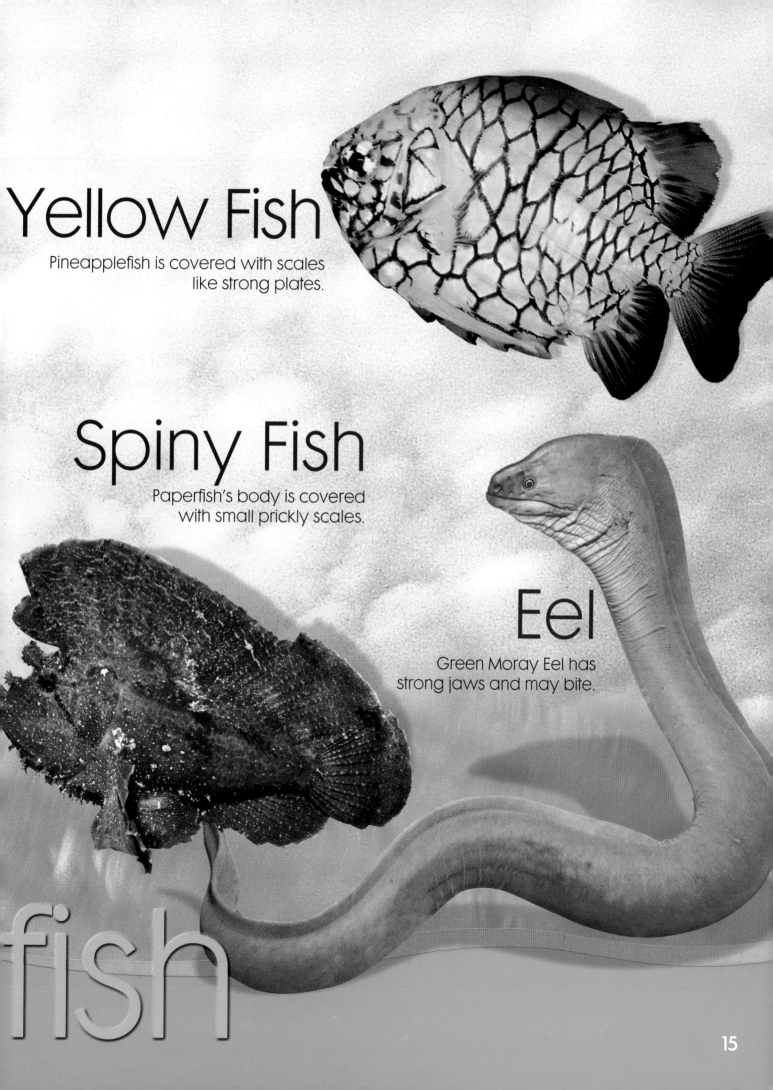

Yellow Fish

Pineapplefish is covered with scales like strong plates.

Spiny Fish

Paperfish's body is covered with small prickly scales.

Eel

Green Moray Eel has strong jaws and may bite.

fish

Jellyfish

Mosaic Sea Jelly is not a strong swimmer but can move itself through the water.

Dolphin

Bottlenose Dolphin sometimes chooses to visit people in shallow water.

Octopus

Octopus has eight legs.

What animals live in Australia?

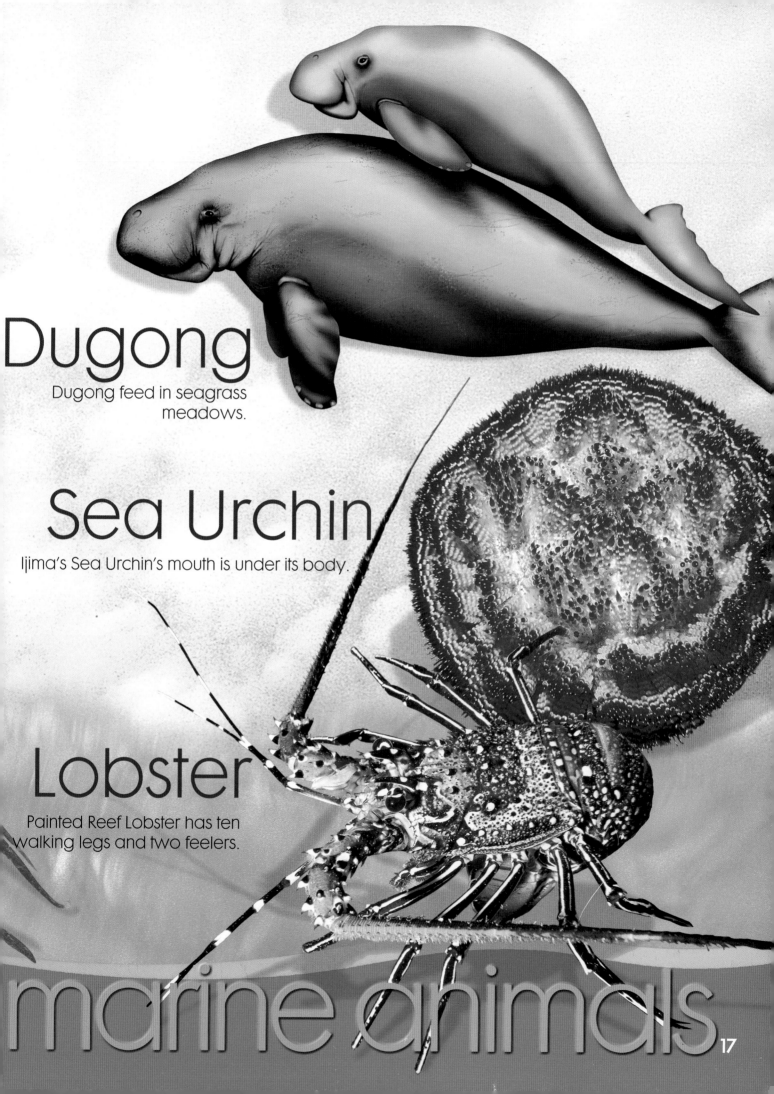

Dugong

Dugong feed in seagrass meadows.

Sea Urchin

Ijima's Sea Urchin's mouth is under its body.

Lobster

Painted Reef Lobster has ten walking legs and two feelers.

marine animals

Parrot

Australian King Parrot feeds mainly on seeds, nuts and berries.

Frog

Red-eyed Tree-frog lives in the topmost branches of rainforest trees.

Where do Australian animals live?

Butterfly

Cairns Birdwing Butterfly was once a caterpillar then a chrysalis.

Possum

Green Ringtail Possum's fur is really white, yellow and black, but looks green.

rainforest

Lyrebird

Superb Lyrebird lives in high rainforest and sings a beautiful song.

Wombat

Common Wombat lives in forest-covered mountains.

Where do Australian animals live

Wallaby

Red-necked Wallaby carries her joey in her pouch where it drinks her milk.

Possum

Mountain Pygmy-possum spends winter asleep (or "hibernating").

high country

Goanna

Goanna (Lace Monitor) is a tree-climber.

Numbat

Numbat has a long sticky tongue for catching termites to eat.

Where do Australian animals live?

Rosella

Crimson Rosella feeds on fruit, seeds and insects.

Kangaroo

Eastern Grey Kangaroo and joey live in mobs that eat bushland grass.

bushland

23

Dingo

Dingo is a wild dog that can live in dry country but it needs water to drink.

Bilby

Bilby lives in dry, hot areas, sheltering in a burrow during the day.

Where do Australian animals live?

Mouse

Spinifex Hopping-mouse comes out from its burrow to feed at night.

Lizard

Thorny Devil can slowly change colour to match wherever it is.

desert

Bird

Eastern Yellow Robin sings at the first light of dawn.

Potoroo

Baby Long-nosed Potoroo stays close to its mother.

Where do Australian animals live?

Gliders

Up to 20 Feathertail Gliders can be found in a nest in a tree hollow.

Snake

Northern Brown Tree Snake hunts lizards, birds and bats at night.

forest

Seagull

Silver Gull lives near the sea and eats sea animals, but will noisily quarrel over food scraps.

Seal

New Zealand Fur-seal pup drinks its mother's rich milk to grow fast.

Where do Australian animals live?

Penguin

Little Penguin nests on southern Australian coasts.

Crabs

Ghost Crabs run quickly over the sand to reach their burrows.

Sea Star

Fire-brick Sea Star has five arms with rows of little tubes underneath that move it along.

Clownfish

Orange-fin Anemonefish lives safely among stinging anemone tentacles.

Where do Australian animals live?

Lionfish

Lionfish has stinging spines.

Reef Fish

Blue Tang swim among branching coral.

Coral Fish

Beaked Coralfish pokes its long beak into cracks in the coral to find food.

reef

Eagle

Wedge-tailed Eagle finds small animals to eat on the grassy plai

Mouse

Plains mouse and baby will run and hide in a burrow.

Where do Australian animals live?

Kangaroo

Red Kangaroo and joey feed on the grass of the plains.

Parrot

Australian Ringneck looks for grass seeds on the ground to eat.

grassy plains

Platypus

Platypus swims to find food in clean waterways.

Frog

Striped Burrowing Frog swim in dams and waterholes.

How do Australian animals behave?

Sea Turtle

Green Turtle spends most of its life swimming in the ocean.

Fish

Emperor Angelfish swim near coral reefs.

swimming

Possum

Long-tailed Pygmy-possum running down the tree trunk has a tail used for gripping.

Bandicoot

Eastern Barred Bandicoot runs quickly when looking for worms, insects and plant bulbs to eat.

How do Australian animals behave?

Tasmanian Devil

Tasmanian Devil runs across a fallen tree trunk.

Goanna

Sand Monitor, or goanna, can run very fast to reach safety.

running

Flying-fox

Spectacled Flying-fox folds its wings and hangs from a branch.

Turtle

Krefft's River Turtle warms its body in the sunshine as it rests on a log.

How do Australian animals behave?

Koala

Koala wedges itself in the fork of a gum tree to sleep.

Wombat

Common Wombat sleeps in a burrow.

resting

Kangaroo

Eastern Grey Kangaroo hops on strong back legs.

Frog

Red-eyed Tree-frog hops to find insects to eat.

hopping

How do Australian animals behave?

Possum

Daintree River Ringtail Possum
lives in rainforest trees.

Gecko

Northern Leaf-tailed Gecko
climbs trees so it can hide
on the bark of a tree trunk.

climbing

Bird

Forest Kingfisher flies back to its nest with food for its chicks.

Bat

Ghost Bat flies on wings made of membrane, which is like layers of thin skin.

flying

How do Australian animals behave?

Parrots

Rainbow Lorikeets preen their feathers before roosting in a tree.

Kookaburra

Laughing Kookaburra fluffs its feathers to keep warm while it roosts during the night.

roosting

Seal

Australian Fur-seals chase fish to eat.

Wallaby

Mareeba Rock-wallaby eats flowers as well as grass.

eating

How do Australian animals behave?

Bird

Eastern Spinebill sips
nectar from a flower.

Dingo

Dingo laps up some
cool, fresh water.

drinking

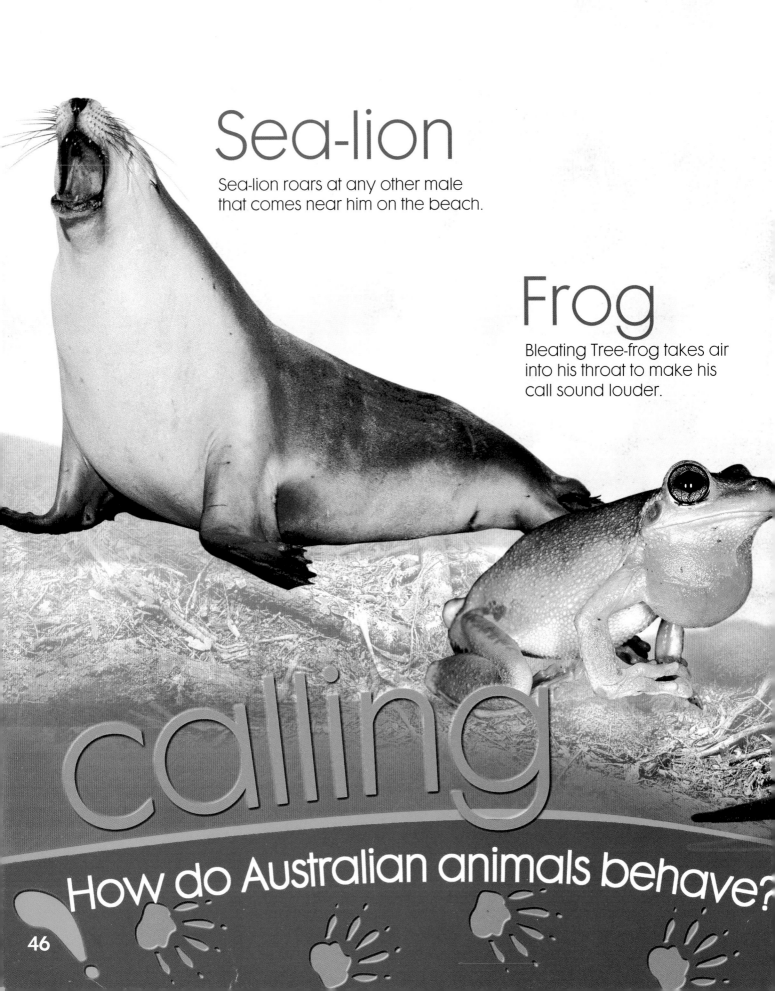

Sea-lion

Sea-lion roars at any other male that comes near him on the beach.

Frog

Bleating Tree-frog takes air into his throat to make his call sound louder.

calling

How do Australian animals behave?

Dolphin

Bottlenose Dolphins are very playful.
They leap from the ocean and
splash back into the water.

Kangaroos

Young Eastern Grey Kangaroos play-fight to
practise for real fights when they grow up.

playing

Birds

Red-tailed Tropicbird scrapes a nest in a sheltered spot on the shore.

Quolls

The female Eastern Quoll lines a nest in her den with grass.

nesting

How do Australian animals behave?